7/9/2023

My Sist

Rosa L. Walker

DISCOVERING

THE

WARRIOR

WIDOW

ROSA L. WALKER

Print ISBN: 978-1-66784-983-6
eBook ISBN: 978-1-66784-984-3

Printed in the United States of America

DEDICATIONS

I dedicate, *Discovering the Warrior Widow* to Jesus Christ. I acknowledge Him in all my ways and achievements as it declares in Provers 3:6, "In all thy ways acknowledge him, And he shall direct thy paths.

I want to acknowledge Prophet Desmond Peterson, Prophetess Ruby Griffith, and Prophetess Cher Bond for their divine obedience to the Holy Spirit and speaking a blessed word of prophecy into my life.

Thank you to the contributing writers: Cher Bond, Charlease Cannon, E. Claudette Freeman, Pecan Tree Publishing and Literary Services, Albert F. Harris, Diane Reid and Robert H. Walker, IV; who shared their valuable perspectives and insights into my story.

This book is dedicated to my children, family, friends, and church members at the Good Samaritan Apostolic Church, Brooklyn, New York, and Christ Temple Apostolic Church, Brownsville, TN.

This book is also dedicated to those in glory, who were mentors and spiritual warriors in my life: Nola Avery, Goldie Becton, Bishop Dewitt Jordan, and Mother Maggie Jordan.

TABLE OF CONTENTS

DEDICATIONS   V

FOREWORD   1

Chapter 1.   A Warrior for God's Will   4

Chapter 2.   Praise God in Every Situation   7

Chapter 3.   My Warrior Widow Story   9

Chapter 4.   A Warrior and Her Soldiers   14

Chapter 5.   Plan for Their Success   18

Chapter 6.   Why God Calls Widows to Be Warriors   20

Chapter 7.   The Exhortation: Rescuing the Wife Inside the Widow   25

Chapter 8.   Warrior Widows Stand Your Watch   31

FINAL THOUGHTS   34

NOTES   37

FOREWORD

How Momma Developed Her Spiritual Foundation

I remember in vivid details the questions that I asked my mother. During those trying early days, after the loss of my father. It was trying because we were suddenly without the strong, male leader of our family. Yet, we began to lean into the mighty strength of our mother and even more in God. My siblings and I needed assurance that all would be well. That our family would continue to thrive, even without the presence of our father.

Raising three children, by herself, in New York City during the 1980s and 1990s was no easy task. There was danger in the streets, on the buses, the subways, and the highways. People were robbed, raped, kidnapped, and murdered daily. In fact, there was always news of child molestation in the city. Car accidents were constant. To say that tumultuous times and occurrences were surrounding a family grieving, is an understatement.

Every day, she would pray that God would grant her traveling mercy; while commuting. She taught her children to do the same. But she also taught her children to pray with faith and trust in God. She taught us the spiritual principles she was resting on and would continue to rely on. As she unfolds her story, I hope that you will develop the faith muscles that made her a warrior widow and conditioned her children to be warriors in their own lives.

Binding the Strongman

This parable of Binding the Strongman Jesus says "how can one enter into a strong man's house, and spoil his goods, except he first binds the strong man?" (Matthew 12:29). My Momma would pray vehemently that the Holy Spirit would protect us.

Favor

Mom was inspired by Joseph and Daniel in the Bible, who were so heavily favored by the kings they served. Despite working around people who were jealous of them and working in an ungodly environment. They were able to thrive. Mom knew in our daily lives favor from God and man was something she and her children would also need. She prayed that God would grant all of us favor. Believing our family could thrive and excel over all our circumstances.

You Have Not, Because You Ask Not

My momma said "Many Christians do not realize that they serve a God who has limitless resources. He is willing to provide those resources to His children." We all find ourselves at a point where there is a lack in our lives that can be related to finances, health, or support. God can address those needs and all we need to do is ask. Christians need to understand that we do not always need to suffer from lack. God has abundant supernatural resources available to us. When we ask Him with a humble heart, not fearing our situation. Momma made sure her children knew God would provide blessings aligned with His will and His purpose for each of us.

Tithes and Offering

Momma always trusted God to provide for our family. After the death of her husband, my dad, she was able to overcome the challenges of her faith. By faith, she would resist the lies of the enemy. These concerns were that there would not be enough. The best example of this resistance was her faithful and cheerful attitude of paying tithes and offerings; despite having only one income in the house. Momma stood on God's promise in St. Luke 6:38 in the Bible. Jesus explains in this scripture when you give, your giving will be returned to you in greater measure than you gave. She taught us II Corinthians 9:6–8, where Paul said "He which soweth sparingly shall reap also sparingly; and he which soweth bountifully shall reap also bountifully." God always honors His Word. I Samuel 15:22, where God tells us that obedience to Him is greater than a sacrifice. My mother's sacrifice and giving spirit was passed down to us, her children.

Reach Out to Witness

Momma demonstrated and spoke words of wisdom (and still does), saying that during times of trials, we can become so bound by our grief and struggles that we forget the people living around us. While Christ was in extreme pain on the cross, His heart was concerned for the eternal souls of men around Him, as written in St. Luke 23:42–43

"And he said unto Jesus, Lord, remember me when thou comest into thy kingdom, And Jesus said unto him, Verily I say unto thee, Today shalt thou be with me in paradise."

Relying upon God's grace during trials can magnify our witness. During the season right after Dad's death, whenever she found herself drowning in the grief of losing her beloved husband. Momma would reach out to other grieving widows with the Gospel of Jesus Christ. She would minister through her pain. She would serve others unselfishly as an example of Jesus Christ. Therefore, God commissioned her to become an evangelist for The Kingdom of God. She is the definition and a glowing example of a warrior widow, one who fights for The Kingdom of God through grief, tears, and pain. She is my momma, Rosa L. Walker.

My siblings and I are glad to be a part of her life and testimony!!!!!!

A Warrior for God's Will

A young woman raised in a small rural Tennessee town grabbed her hopes and dreams, and shortly after graduating from high school, she headed to one of the most active cities in America – New York. That young woman was me! Leaving Tennessee was exciting, invigorating, intimidating, and would cause me to pull on every fiber of trust in God that I had.

When I arrived in New York in 1962, the Big Apple was much broader in cultures, social concerns, community dynamics, criminal activity, and more than I had experienced in Brownsville. Soon after stepping foot on the concrete jungle of New York; I was employed by a delightful Jewish family. I worked for them for three months as a nanny. My cousin Goldie Becton asked me to leave my job as a nanny and come live with her. She encouraged me to start working with her at a city hospital. I listen to her advice and was hired as a nurse's aide. My cousin Goldie introduced me to a closer relationship with God—a relationship that wonderfully included being filled with the Holy Spirit.

Later on, I met Robert H. Walker Jr and we were married in 1971. During our marriage, we had four children: Rosalind, Goldie, Robert III (whom we lost in 1976), and then Robert Walker, IV. The loss of a child was devastating. It created a void that I cannot describe. Painfully, I understand what others mean when they say no parent should ever have to bury a child—under any circumstances. I experienced such deep loss again when my husband, Robert Jr., died in 1981.

Robert Jr's death made me a member of a global community. It is a community of women who wail out of sorrow grief without warning, find strength in their pain, and find purpose in losing a beloved spouse. None of us who became widows volunteered for this new lifestyle, yet God allowed it and chose us. *Discovering The Warrior Widow* is my living testimony of what God has done for me through my placement in widowhood. Through my experience, I hope to provide encouragement, comfort, and peace for you through your widow's grief journey. My story is based on the power of prayer in my life and becoming a warrior widow. A warrior recognizes God's power, purposes, and providence. It is my testimony of faith, perseverance and prayer that changed my course in life. God became my provider. He did amazing things for my children and me. He can do the same for you.

My favorite scripture that I leaned on for strength down through the years is Psalm 34:1, "I will bless The Lord at all times; His praise shall continually be in my mouth." Not only is this book a testimony of my personal life, but it has been written to motivate and encourage others. For everyone experiencing the misfortune of losing a spouse and trying to raise children alone. I hope pastors, funeral directors, and healthcare providers would refer to this book as a powerful resource for Christian counseling. Regardless of your devastating circumstances, God sees, knows, and He cares. He has the power to deliver you from pain and suffering, and to hold you until your wardrobe of sorrow is replaced with the garments of joy.

Discovering the warrior as a widow caused me to lean on life lessons and strengthen my faith in God. These experiences extended the ministry to others that I needed in my own life. Discovering the warrior as a widow meant learning to fight and intercede for my family and position my children to do the same. Discovering the warrior as a widow has meant allowing God to re-order my steps through devastating loss and trusting Him. There is a divine purpose for you as a widow or widower, and it begins with being a warrior!

Rosa Walker

Praise God in Every Situation

Job, a man whom the Bible says, "he sinned not nor blamed God foolishly" (Job 1:22) lost all of his material possessions, children, livestock, and his health deteriorated. Eventually, he lost his desire to live. The loss was like a roaring tsunami in Job's life. In a brief, sudden period, his life was turned upside down. Without warning, death, loss, and grief overwhelmed his daily manner of living. The loss happened just like that!

Job was one of the richest men of his time, yet tragedy did not evade him. Loss and death have no respecter of person or status. To add to Job's woes, his beloved wife pressured him to curse God and die, but Job kept his faith in God. (Job 2:9)

Some of us may have the same, if not a similar, attitude as Job's wife. How could God allow one of his servants to endure numerous, unpredictable tragedies for no apparent reason? How could Job not question God? Fortunately, we know the conversation between God and Satan that Job himself was unaware of knowing. Satan was the master-mind—with God's approval and staunch boundaries—behind all of Job's calamities. Yet God trusted Job to remain a humble and faithful servant. Job's love for God was deeper than his devastating situation. He trusted God's intentions.

Widows and widowers understand the significant pain Job endured. Even if sickness was present, death brings a sudden atmosphere of finality. We often focus more on our situation without giving thought to what God is doing behind the scenes. We may not always agree with God's methods, but His thoughts are not our thoughts, and His ways are not our ways (Isaiah 55:8). God sees the bigger picture, and like Job, we should not hurry to blame God, but trust His plans for us.

When the shroud of death hangs over widow or widowers. We can be caught up in thinking that we are in control of our lives. For example: Our careers are established. our finances are in good- shape and our health, thus far, has not given us any major trouble. Death makes us keenly and powerfully aware of how fleeting all those things can be.

In the midst of our grief, we sadly realize that we have met a sorrowful line in the marriage vows—until death do us part. Even though, unexpected situations pop up in our lives. We often wonder how we will make it through. We might find ourselves questioning God; why me? In that place of realization, we take inventory of our life. We ponder whether we were grateful for our spouse. Did we thank God for the achievements and challenges that He brought us through in our marriages? We must remind ourselves of God's love for us and the promises He has given us.

Even in despair; widows must remember to praise God for what He has done, is currently doing, and will do for us in the future. We must learn the true meaning of praising God because our circumstances can quickly turn from good to worse.

When we praise God— through sorrowful experiences—we will rejoice as Job did. "So the LORD blessed the latter end of Job more than his beginning: for he had fourteen thousand sheep, and six thousand camels, and a thousand yoke of oxen, and a thousand she asses (Job 42:12)."

CHAPTER ONE

My Warrior Widow Story

Certainly, none of us thinks about being called to a widowhood as part of our life's purpose or vision. Yet, some will experience it and learn how to navigate the new dimensions of life that being a widow brings.

I met my future husband, Robert H. Walker, Jr., in 1965. I was living in New York and was focused on my education. His sister, Etta Lane and I attended Central School of Practical Nursing together. She introduced me to Robert. I liked him because he was very quiet and well-mannered. He had so much patience with me and others. He was thirteen years older than me. Therefore, he had experienced more in life than me. I also admired that he loved his family, and he actively showed his love for them. He spent a lot of quality time with his nieces and nephews, taking them out to eat and doing things they loved doing. He had two brothers and three sisters. Each brother was in their second marriage. Robert intentionally spent time with the kids from his brothers' first marriages. He wanted all his nieces and nephews to know that their uncle loved them dearly and they also loved him. His dedication to his family was attractive to me. Family warmth, responsibility, and commitment were a big deal for me. Big family ties were something we shared together.

Robert was six feet tall, slim and handsome. Even though he was physically attractive, the biggest attraction for me was his quiet demeanor. Another quality about Robert that I loved. He didn't have the behavior problem that my father did. My father would drink heavily on the weekend. His alcoholism would get on my last nerve growing-up. Robert didn't drink at all. Boy, I was like a pig in mud when I discovered that.

We dated for six years. I'm here to tell you, I wasn't in any hurry to get married, coming from a large family. Even though, he was older than me; he patiently waited until I was ready to get married. Robert knew that, and he respected that. I appreciated him the more because he did. The funny thing is he proposed to me six months after we started dating. We met in 1965; that Christmas, he asked if he could give me an engagement ring! Of course, I said, "NO WAY!"

I was determined not to get married to anyone until my education was completed. If the marriage didn't go well, I would be able to earn a living and take care of myself. That was necessary wisdom for me. Therefore, I earned a certificate of completion from the Central School of Practical Nursing in 1965. I graduated from Queensborough Community College with an Associate's Degree in Applied Science in 1970.

Becoming an RN, I gained financially and professionally. As an RN, the nursing skills that I learned in college was advantageous to me. I applied those skills to provide optimal comprehensive care to my patients. As an RN, my family, friends and church members would occasionally call me and ask for my medical opinion. Many of them would ask for prayer for their health conditions. As an RN, my occupation allotted me a middle-class lifestyle. While my free time was spent dating Robert and enjoying it immensely. He loved dining out, his favorite dish was filet mignon. He also loved going to the movies and attending Broadway plays. Robert and I agreed to get married on January 24th, 1971; because I had completed my Associate's Degree.

We started our family immediately. He loved spending time with his children, taking them to the park, movies, and The Bronx Zoo. I would take the children shopping with me. They had a lot of fun picking-out their individual boxes of cereal. Parenting was an important blessing for both Robert and me. He was a strong, wonderful provider and a present father. Robert and I made sure every week our children had to show us their completed Sunday school assignment.

Our main dreams for our children were to receive the best education possible. We talked about preparing them for college; even while they were far from it. Robert and I decided to send our children to private schools; because we wanted them to have a positive, productive learning experience.

Robert and I would find our faith tested in a most traumatic way, the death of a child. Such disappointment and despair grasped me, while the pain weighed heavily on Robert. My medicine for coping was to get busy and involved in church ministries. I had the time to do so because I was still on maternity leave. After being off work for two months, my best day was—believe it or not—when I went back to work. I felt like a brand-new person getting back into the routine of the Intensive Care Unit (ICU). What a difference I felt that first day! This was the perfect place for me.

Robert H. Walker, III was born February 3rd, 1976. He was a hydrocephalic, what is known more commonly as a Waterhead baby. As defined by the National Institute of Neurological Disorders and Strokes, Hydrocephalus is "an abnormal buildup of fluid in the ventricles (cavities) deep within the brain. This excess fluid causes the ventricles to widen, putting pressure on the brain's tissues."

The surgeon decided to treated my infant son with the surgical placement of a shunt system. According to the National Institute of Neurological Disorders and Strokes, "This system diverts the flow of CSF from a site within the central nervous system to another area of the body where it can be absorbed as part of the circulatory process." Robert and I knew our son had a low life expectancy and the substantial risk of meningitis. However, there was a blessing that Robert III's Apgar score was eight; the perfect score is ten. Even with that, our little son died one month later, on March 3rd. Devastation is the tip of the iceberg for what we felt. To this day, on February 3rd, I remember his birthday.

Though I experienced every stage of grief with my son's death, I cannot say that it prepared me for my husband's death. In losing our son, I had his father, my husband, to hold onto. Though we grieved separately in our own ways. We still shared a powerful loss that we could be present to help each other through. Unfortunately, that story did not support my widow's story.

Robert Jr.'s death was sudden. He had a massive heart attack on the job. I can only imagine that he was working and talking with co-workers about the news of the day and the baseball game. When the paramedics arrived, there was nothing they could do. He was simply gone. How I found-out about Robert's death on the job. The police came to my house and informed me. My cousin Nola drove me to his job; so that I could drive his car back home. I did not get the opportunity to sit with him in a hospital. Nor did I have the opportunity to hold him as his wife.

Devastation struck me again. Yet, my faith in God sustained me. I knew I could depend on God and His Word. God would not forsake me. I still had to find my way through this new world. I was in the world of widowhood. A woman gripped in grief. It was then that I found and read a book that explained the five stages of grieving. I realized I'd been through some of those stages before. Surely, I was moving through most of them again. But I was determined to manage my life of grief productively. So that, I could be whatever my children were going to need me to be. I attended a seminar on death and dying, and I occupied myself with outreach ministry, fasting and praying. A year after his death, the children and I sought counseling, which was a wonderful balm in the healing process.

Strangely, one of the things that helped sustain me after Robert's death was part of his character. My husband was a good leader and provider. And now I had to step-up in that role. Initially, it was a bit intimidating, but God reminded me that He had instilled leadership skills in me. God had strategically made me the oldest of thirteen siblings. He positioned me to help take care of my siblings; while my parents worked or shopped. My childhood had prepared me for what I was going to experience in life.

Robert had a strong interpersonal relationship with his children; he often spent quality time with them together and individually. Robert took them to the movies, park, zoo and museums. I had to understand that I was not the only one who had lost a precious gift; they had too.

CHAPTER TWO

A Warrior and Her Soldiers

One of the greatest concerns of a widow with a family is – her children. Lifestyle adjustments abound. There is no more division of duties. Suddenly, you find yourself doing all of the things with the kids the other parent used to do and realizing that it is not the same.

When Robert Jr. died, my oldest daughter, Rosalind, was ten years old, and my other daughter Goldie was nine, and my son Robert IV was two and ½ years old. The girls missed their father terribly. One of the things they missed most was going to the movies.

I thank God for wise counsel in my life. After my husband's death, I would pay one of my friend's sons to take them to the movies. I was trying to fulfill the void of their father's death. Another friend listened to what I had done, and while she understood, she advised me to reconsider my decision. She stated paying someone to take the children to the movies "is not a good idea." Your husband did that with the children. Let them remember those moments as quality time with him. She went on to say, "Let that be a time that they always look back and remember—this is what we did with Dad. She was right, I had to allow them to mourn losing their dad in their own way. However, after we started counseling and they were able to express their grief in a safe environment and healthy manner. The harshness of mourning passed over.

I was a single woman with three children about to enter critical ages in New York City. There was a world of negative incentives, enticements, and dangers that the enemy could have easily drawn them into. A life of addiction, imprisonment, violence or legal troubles was not what their dad and I dreamed of or desired for our children.

I had to be certain and vigilant about instilling God and acknowledging Him in their lives every day. I remembered how the atmosphere in my cousin Goldie's two-story, the two-family house was always electrified with the energy of God. So, I did what I could to keep that atmosphere strong in our home. Prayer, fasting, reading The Word of God, and speaking The Word of God were regular practices.

Seeking God's wisdom requires a daily relationship with Him. God will direct you and give you the answers you need if you pray, fast, and read His Word. Remember what God's Word says, and tell Him, "I believe Your Word for myself and my children." Parenting can be an emotionally stressful experience. A single parent needs to seek God's wisdom first to make the best decision for his or her children. "If any of you lack wisdom, let him ask of God, that giveth to all men (James 1:5).

My children had to say their prayers every morning and every night. I stressed that no matter where they are, where they go, what they do in life. They were never to forget to acknowledge God; who gives us peace, joy, and love. They needed to know that El Shaddai, (God Almighty), would always be there for them. They needed to know Jehovah Jireh (Provider). Though my father was a heavy drinker on the weekend, he was a fabulous provider. I never knew a hungry day in my life.

Like my father, my husband was a fabulous provider. I wanted to prepare my children to be productive adults and be great stewards of their lives and money. Robert and I were dedicated parents to our children. In our home, we emulated II Thessalonians 3:10: "For even when we were with you, this we commanded you, that if any would not work, neither should he eat." When my daughters and son turned 14 years old and could obtain work permits, they got jobs.

I trained them how to outline their responsibilities. After tithing, the rule in our family was you must save. I told them "Do not blow your entire paycheck."

"Praise God for His provision and His promises to take care of you. I was an example of this. It is something single parents (all parents) should demonstrate. God's children should pay their tithes and offerings because in His Word (Malachi 3:10) requires it. Single parents should (like I did) openly discuss financial matters and the importance of giving God the first fruits. Then, praise Him when God meets your family's needs according to His riches and glory!"

When I got ready to pay my bills (car payments, utilities, insurance, private school tuition, and everything else). Several times a year, I would sit the children down and go over the monthly budget. Dining-out at restaurants; we enjoyed being together as a family. We ate out at least twice a month. If the money became short, we would have to cut back a little bit. We never sacrificed what was set aside for God. I consistently reinforced the importance of paying your tithes and offerings to the church, no matter how difficult the financial struggle might be.

I sacrifice to send the children to private schools. Their dad knew that a college education was certain for each of them. The quality of education at private schools would better prepare them for college. I did not want them to struggle with their education as I did. While I did well in nursing school, succeeding academically was not easy.

The educational system in the part of Tennessee, where I was raised was horrible. When I moved to New York, I enrolled in night classes in a high school in The Bronx. I chose to take English classes to strengthen my writing skills. I had to study twice as hard as everyone else in the class to get my assignments done. The teachers in my hometown did the best they could, but I struggled as a student in New York City. So, I sent my children to private school, so that their academic foundation would be strong. God heard and answered my prayers for my young children. They all accepted Jesus Christ into their lives. He created a wall of blessings around them. Two of them have master's degrees, and one has a master's degree and a Juris Doctor. I am grateful that they are all still actively serving The Lord.

Part of the successful plan for my family was to keep the children involved in activities: church ministry, athletics, and developmental programs. This promoted healthy and proper decision-making skills. They took piano lessons. My son took Karate. My daughters participated in Girl Scouts. Every summer, they were in camp. In addition, the children spent time in church ministries. "Train up a child in the way he should go and when he is old, he will not depart from it." (Proverbs 22:6)

God blessed Robert and I with a wonderful family. We desired that our children would be successful in their endeavors, well-educated and good people. Psalm 127: 4-5 "As arrows are in the hand of a mighty man; so are children of the youth. Happy is the man that hath his quiver full of them."

Fill your home environment with The Word of God. Create and maintain an atmosphere of worship in your home. Spend quality time with your children. Make sure that time includes: prayer, reading The Word of God, and encouraging them to ask questions about the Word of God. Anoint and pray with your children daily. Make no mistake, the enemy is after them, but it is the power of God that will guard and protect them.

CHAPTER THREE

Plan for Their Success

Assuring a positive and productive livelihood for my kids and me was paramount, after my husband's sudden death. However, there were days grief was present. Pre-planning for me became a necessity in creating the victory that God promised. I had the amazing and yet intimidating responsibility to raise two girls and one boy on my own. In that responsibility, I decided and proposed that we would not fail, we would not succumb to overwhelming negative influences. As a widow, I had to acknowledge that my co-parent was gone.

Children are aware of the loss of a parent, particularly when that parent was an integral part of the family structure. In our family, their father was the stabilizer. He stepped up and stepped in to oversee whatever needed managing. It was contingent on me, during my planning, to be aware of the psychological and physical needs of my children. Our loss left me with storms of swirling questions. Am I going to be able to manage without my husband? Will I be able to manage financially? Should I go back home where I will have help? What about school? Am I going to be able to continue working? What am I going to do when my children become teenagers? The questions consumed me. Yet, I realized that the questions helped me identify what needed to go into a coherent and comprehensive plan. With each question, I could outline what steps or options existed. I could then weigh those against the children's needs and my own.

My three young children were not cognizant of the permanency of death. Children do not understand that the absence of the person causes inevitable changes to life.

Communicating with the kids at an age-appropriate level helped navigate those intricacies of death. It was also contingent upon me to involve my three children in my planning efforts to ensure a successful outcome. This team family approach, I believe, helped me assure them that things would be fine, and it helped them express their concerns and desires in our new normal. As a working single parent of three, it was important that I didn't let my family suffer, nor my work performance deteriorate. Faced with this reality, I needed to organize and prioritize a schedule for our lives. Thereby, no one in the family would feel neglected.

When odds are against you, it is easy to find yourself in a state of deep depression. Planning helped prevent depression by including spiritual routines for the children and me. We prayed, read the Bible and discussed the Word of God together. I knew that I was a child of the living God and believed that He would supply my every need. Therefore, my first step in our plan was depend upon God for guidance. I confessed to The Lord that, I am weak and I needed Him more than ever. (Isaiah 40:29)

Like the saints of old, I knew that I had work to do. The Lord heard my cries and our prayers and provided me with the strength and will to overcome the insurmountable odds. I thank God for my natural family and my church family, who embraced and supported us. The Savior's arms comforted us through it all.

CHAPTER FOUR

Why God Calls Widows to Be Warriors

"About 700,000 women become a widow in the U.S. each year. There are 258,000,000 widows worldwide. Almost half of them live in extreme poverty, and many are subject to cruel violence. There are 13.6 million widows in America." These statistics from walk with a widow.com prove an alarming growing community of widows globally. God's heart is toward those who grieve the loss of a spouse. They have experienced a difficult line in the marital vows – until death does us part.

There are Biblical scriptures admonishing the body of Christ to be supportive to widow.

James 1:27 "Pure religion and undefiled before God and the Father is this, to visit the fatherless and widows in their affliction."

Psalms 82:3 "Defend the poor and fatherless: Do justice to the afflicted and needy."

Acts 6:1 "And in those days, when the number of the disciples was multiplied, there arose a murmuring of the Grecians against the Hebrews, because their widows were neglected in the daily ministration."

Exodus 22:22-23 "Ye shall not afflict any widow, or fatherless child. If thou afflict them in any wise, and they cry at all unto Me, I will surely hear their cry.

The King James Dictionary of Studylight.org defines WARRIOR as a noun. 1. In a general sense, a soldier is a man engaged in military life. 2. Emphatically, a brave man, a good soldier.

A widow warrior does not condemn death, because she knows that it is a part of life. A widow warrior puts on the whole armour of God for spiritual warfare. "Above all, taking the shield of faith, wherewith ye shall be able to quench all the fiery darts of the wicked." (Ephesians 6: 16)

God elevated me after my husband's death. That statement might strike you as odd unless you are a fellow widow warrior. A widow warrior understands that the loss of a spouse does not mean we descend into bleakness, but—if we trust God—we ascend into the assignment. While I was doing ministry at home as a single parent; God had others I would need to administer to and serve. My pastor asked me to become the supervisor of the financial staff at church. I became a Sunday School senior class teacher. I became active in teaching a Home-Bible Study Course, which lead many people to Christ. That's why God calls widow warriors – to help build The Kingdom of God and sharpen His disciples.

My obedient service propelled me to become a warrior widow because it presented opportunities for me to share my testimony. I found that God used what He had imparted in me to help widows and comfort single parents to live for God. I encouraged and instructed them on what God could do for themselves and their children. Some of that encouragement was as simple as emphasizing the importance of attending church as a family. While gently inspiring them to serve and assist others. The widow warrior in me saw another reason God calls us, to help nurture families in development.

God was using His Holy Spirit in me to comfort others. While, I was working in ICU one day the nursing supervisor sent for me. A young nurse had lost her newborn and was discouraged. The supervisor said, "Rosa, you've lost a newborn. You should be able to comfort her. Because the nurses and doctors can't calm her down. She won't listen or talk to anyone.

I started praying as I ran up to the recovery room. I took a deep breath. She was lying in bed with the TV blasting. I walked over to her and said, "Oh, stop that crying. I lost my newborn son. He only lived one month." She turned off the TV (when other people tried to talk to her, she would turn the volume up louder). She sat up in the bed and looked directly into my eyes. I shared the tragedy of losing my newborn son with her. She started asking me questions about my baby. Her interaction with me was very rewarding. The next day, she was discharged from the hospital. She had a new attitude and a happier outlook on life. As I embraced her, I told her, "Girl, get busy and get yourself another baby." My story of pain was similar to hers. My testimony helped give hope back into her spirit. That is why God calls widow warriors.

I must tell you that her experience, reminded me of how someone else testimony comforted me, during my dilemma. When the doctor told me and my husband that our son was a hydrocephalic. (Waterhead baby) I cried for several hours. Nothing anyone said or did could stop my tears from falling. I prayed at that moment that God would take my life. I said, "Lord when I inhale, the best thing you could do for me is not let me exhale. Just kill me now!"

God wanted me to stop the pity party. A nurse came in to visit me, and she proceeded to console me. "Rosa, stop this nonsense." I stopped crying long enough to wonder who she was and to hear what she thought she could tell me. She continued, "I know why you're crying. You're crying because your baby is a hydrocephalic. You think he will be mentally challenged. And you think that when you die, who will take care of him? All of this is nonsense, you've got two kids and a husband. You need to get up and start living right now!"

She surely had my attention. Her next statement confirmed that God sent her specifically to me. She went on to say, "I am an LPN and a hydrocephalic. When I took the nursing board exam, I passed it the first time. My Apgar score was seven and your son's Apgar score is eight. Stop all that crying. Ask your doctor to transfer your newborn to the hospital; where my neurosurgeon works. Let him put a shunt in your son's head. Continue to move on in life with your family. I didn't shed another tear.

At that moment, I needed someone whose testimony could relate to my situation. This is what the LPN story did for me. Her testimony gave me hope. As I reflect, my testimony helped to encourage the young nurse and gave her hope.

I walked by faith and not by sight. That was my sword – His Word. Often, I quote this scripture: "Thy word is a lamp unto my feet. And a light unto my path." (Psalm 119:105) And I live that truth still today. God calls the warrior widow to remind generations of who The Savior of the world sincerely is.

A warrior was always within me. I lived with my Cousin Goldie in her two-story family house for seven years. She poured into my life naturally and spiritually. She took me to the human resources department on her job to fill-out an application. Once hired, that job at the city hospital helped propel my nursing career. Cousin Goldie introduced me to Bishop Dewitt and Mother Maggie Jordan, her pastor and his wife at Good Samaritan Apostolic Church. They were all strong examples of holiness and righteousness. The Good Samaritan Apostolic Church family was a community of Holy Ghost-filled believers that lived by faith and not by sight! My Cousin Goldie influenced my life and so many others. She was a great missionary. She traveled to Africa, Haiti, and other foreign countries on mission trips; concerning the Gospel of Jesus Christ.

My Cousin Goldie and Nola, her daughter strongly taught me that when you have trials and tribulations, they only come to make you a better person. They said "God sees something in your personality, attitude, or character that needs to be corrected." And I learned to fortify myself in The Word of God. God may give you a test to work out your flaws. He desires to see you work out your salvation.

God calls widow warriors to be good listeners; for those who are grieving. You can't do that if you don't tune in with your natural and spiritual ears. Never listen with words of judgment and condemnation on your lips. When someone is oppressed and suppressed, they want to withdraw. Your role is to uplift them with The Word of God. Remind them to keep moving and keep going. I always encourage grievers with this scripture, "They that wait upon The Lord strength shall be renewed. They shall mount up with wings of eagles. Run and not get weary, walk and not faint." (Isaiah 40:31) God calls His widow warriors to be His wings on the Earth. He needs you to be obedient to His Word.

CHAPTER FIVE

The Exhortation:
Rescuing the Wife Inside the Widow

Dear wailing, warrior wife inside, I implore you to study the Word of God to get you through your season of grief. While you are reading the scriptures; God will send His Holy Spirit, The Comforter. The Holy Spirit will soothe and remind you; that you are not alone The Holy Spirit will also work in the hearts of people to pour into your life. James 1:27 "Pure religion and undefiled before God and the Father is this, to visit the fatherless and widows in their affliction."

In the book of Ruth, you will find Naomi. She, along with her husband, Elimelech, and their two sons left their country, Bethlehem-Judah, and sojourned to the country of Moab.

Naomi's husband, Elimelech died, and Naomi was left with two sons. The life that she had once known was no more. She was left in a land of idolatry with her two sons and two daughters-in-law. Without hesitation, she would have to walk by faith and not by sight. She would have to lead the family onward and upward. When her two sons died, Naomi had to face their widows and help them make the best decisions for their life. One daughter-in-law, Orpah, returned to her family. Ruth decided she would remain with Naomi. God ordered Naomi and Ruth steps to family members in Bethlehem-Judah. Naomi, an older widow, introduced Ruth, a young widow, to the God she served. She would help position Ruth to become a wife again. Boaz said unto the elders, and unto all the people, "Ye are witnesses this day, that I have bought all that was Elimelech's, and all that was Chilion's and Mahlon's (Naomi's sons). Moreover, Ruth the Moabitess, the wife of Mahlon, have I purchased to be my wife (Ruth 4:9-10)

Once upon a time, I was a wife, but I lost my husband, and now I am a widow. No, I did not give up on my marriage, but I lost my husband. Why did that have to take place? I was happy being a wife, a mother, and most importantly, a Christian. But the time came for me to give up something or someone I loved. How often I had to sit and comfort the wife inside. As a widow, I had to learn how to speak caring and reassuring words to the wife inside. After all the dreams that she had for her family and future had suddenly vanished away. A blissful wife dreads the idea of being viewed as a widow. Although death is inevitable, it is the suddenness that seizes the senses and paralyzes picture-perfect martial partnerships forever. How can one rescue the wife inside the widow? She now lives as a mother by day and a widow with memories of being a wife by night. When everything has quieted down and the children are asleep. She goes to prep dinner for the next day and forgets that she is preparing for four instead of five.

Morning after morning, she rises to the reality of seeing only one pillow pressed with puckers and wrinkles. The other side is the same as it was the night before. Once again, she takes a punch from the fist of pain and attempts to swing back with the power of prayer. As she sojourns to work, she is trailed by tears and anxiety. Although attempts to comfort her are plenteous, she only feels the discomfort and agony of her loss. Perhaps the children will be of comfort to her. Maybe one can comfort her with their father's walk, the other with his smile, or another with his sense of humor. Yes, maybe?

Nevertheless, the widow must take control, move forward, and face the transformation and its challenges head-on! The widow must be aware that the wife inside of her, cannot survive without spiritual intervention. Her body is weak, her knees are feeble, and her heart is heavy. Nonetheless, the widow will say to the wife inside, "Do not fear dear sister. I will teach you everything you need to know. I will persevere in the power of the Holy Spirit. The grace of God will be our gravity and ground. We will not fail. We will not fall. He will bring liberation to you."

You must remember that your Heavenly Father watches you throughout your journey. Psalm 68:5 states: "A father of the fatherless and judge of the widows is God in his holy habitation." Many fears and trepidations overshadow a wife's heart when one becomes a widow, Loneliness will entice and challenge you. Nevertheless, know assuredly that God has granted grace to all, especially widows.

God alone will be your defender and avenger. For He knows the evil, you must endure and the impure imaginations you must cast down. You must bring every thought into captivity and submit it unto The Lord. Ideas will come, and ways to get wealth could influence you. Nevertheless, you must pray as you have always done. Call upon the name of Jesus with your children. Teach them to lean on The Lord for safekeeping.

I Timothy 5:5 reads, "Now she that is a widow indeed, and desolate, trusteth in God, and continueth in supplications and prayers night and day."

The one thing you should always remember is to stand by The Word and know that you do not have to leave God to have success. As a widow, Satan will come to destroy your confidence in God. Therefore, you must remember that God is Holy at all times. There is absolutely no way to make it without prayers and faith. Prayer will grant you the support and stability needed to maintain a virtuous lifestyle. When things do not go right, you must entreat The Lord and fast. Prayer and faith are spiritual weapons that a widow can use to make moral choices; because she is lonely.

Speak to yourself often. Say Dear Wife inside; you must trust God to keep you alive.

Whatever you do, do not doubt God. If God says He is going to do something for you, He anticipates that you will believe Him. When going through your trials and tribulations, please know that God is building up the entire family.

When things get rough; you have to wait upon The Lord to renew your strength. (Isaiah 40:31) As you walk the widow's way, you must understand that God is fine-tuning you. You will realize that you were learning something through the struggle in due season. You will meet others who need strength and comfort as they sojourn through their struggle. You must understand that change will come because you know God. Therefore, learn to be patient with The Lord. Hannah was like you. She had opposition. She had troubles and problems. Hannah longed for years to have a child. In her travailing with that dilemma, we read in First Samuel 1, that she was mocked by Peninnah, her husband Elkanah's other wife, who was able to birth children. Like Hannah, the warrior widow must remain steadfast in the faith, committing and dedicating her prayers to God and continue to press your way. One of the first things you will be tempted to do when you have trouble is contemplating withdrawing.

Dear wife, you will feel the need to withdraw from society. Oftentimes, wives reminisce about life before becoming a widow. Friends often surround you with laughter and conversation. However, when you become a widow, associates who once encircled you with jests and giggles now secretly wonder about your stability and future. Still, some recognize the widow's affliction and begin to minister to the wife inside. Some people will come as supporters with words of reassurance, while others will only smile and embrace you with a gentle hug. Often this type of support is far greater than any words. It demonstrates that someone understands that no words that can heal a shattered heart.

Nonetheless, you must make a good decision to continue to serve The Lord. One of your greatest assets is joy. Joy is a fruit of the Holy Spirit and the joy of The Lord is our strength. You will have to resist the devil and remind him that Jesus defeated him on the cross. Peninnah ridiculed Hannah, but she did not stop going to The Lord's House of Prayer. As you are going through your trials and tribulations, you must always give God praise. Raising your children in these volatile times can be complex.; the Holy Spirit is your lifeline and support. You will need Jesus to be fortified in the Word of God. Reading The Word and devoting time before The Savior should be a daily priority.

The widow should declare the scripture: "The blessings of The Lord, it maketh rich, and he addeth no sorrow with it." (Proverbs 10:22)

You have lost your spouse, and now you are left alone to defend, protect, and provide for your children. Know that your finances will fluctuate; nevertheless, you must remember that you must persevere through prayer. Do not pray alone during your time of lack. Gather your children, inform them of the circumstances and invite them into the prayer. You will teach your children the necessity of entreating The Lord by doing this. The scriptures encourage the reader to--"...train up a child in the way he should go: and when he is old, he will not depart from it." (Proverbs 22:6)

The accountability of the family's future is upon your shoulders now. You have invested your time, energy, and money into your children. In doing so, you will one day reap the benefits of the seed sown.

The widow should understand that tears are inevitable; but you can bring your heart back to peace. When struggling with doubt and disappointment, talk with your Heavenly Father. It is important to understand that tears are inevitable, but you can bring your heart back to peace. When struggling with doubt and disappointment, talk with your Heavenly Father. Nevertheless, stand strong and bold in your faith. Jesus Christ is your faith. Matthew 11:28 reads, Jesus cried out and said, "Come unto me, all ye that labor and are heavy laden, and I will give you rest."

For that reason, when life demands more than you can supply, find Jesus. He will be there waiting to help you carry your heavy burdens. On His shoulders, you can lean on forever and ever, Amen.

CHAPTER SIX

Warrior Widows Stand Your Watch

Becoming a widow, while the mother of three young children and after the death of a child, was horrific. The enemy could have had his way with me amid such darkness, devastation, grief and pain. As he was marching around the Earth seeking someone to devour, I was an excellent candidate for destruction. Except – God had His Hand on me. God had chosen me for the assignment of widowhood. Though the weight often felt overwhelming, He trusted that I could and would bear it. He had prepared me for it through various life lessons.

The precious widow warrior was created to withstand the trials, rejection, pain, bitterness and despair. She overcomes these challenges with the "sword" (The Word of God). You are a warrior called to create a life-changing edification and exhortation movement; for those whose pain you know well. You are a widow warrior—by design.

After marrying Robert H. Walker Jr.; having a family, losing a one-month-old son, and the sudden death of my husband. God has blessed me to raise and educate three children. Presently, they are all serving the Lord. God kept me through my nursing career; that I loved for 40 years in the same hospital in New York and 21 of those years were in CCU.

At age 60, I moved back to Tennessee to be closer to my mother and siblings. I did not move back home to sit on a porch in a rocking chair, though that is a wonderful way to relax. Instead, God put me to work. My life is a testimony to who God is and His power. As a warrior, I have to be available to be used by God.

God gave me trials. I lost my father in September 1980; I lost my husband the following year July 1981. People knew the relationship that I had with God was real. Because they could see the evidence of His power working through me. I can comfort people who have experienced: the death of a child and the sharp pain of instantaneous death. I can do it because a significant part of my ministry has come by walking through the valley of shadow of death and knowing—without a doubt—that God is my shield, my strength, and my strong tower.

The ministry of testimony is the most pertinent reason I wrote this book. Writing one sentence of a book was the furthest thing from my mind. English was my weakest subject in school. Thirty-five years ago in Queens, New York, Prophet Desmond Peterson prophesied that God wanted me to tell my story about being a widow with children. Prophet Peterson was clear in his prophecy, "God has not blessed your children the way He has, nor has He blessed you affluently by happenstance. He wants you to let people know that if they serve Him, what He will do for you and others. And even in a huge city, like New York, God blessed you and your family. Ten years later in Brooklyn, New York, Prophetess Ruby Griffith declared that God would have me write my testimony. After I retired and moved back home to Tennessee. Prophetess Cher Bond in 2019 prophesied to me. She said "Have you thought about writing?" The Lord said "Write your story."

The prophecies were consistent: "The Lord said, write the story." "Sister Walker, have you ever thought of writing your story?" "The Lord said, write." God needed this widow warrior; and He needs you.

Through all the roads that life's journey has taken me, I knew my assignment – glorify God in and through all things. All things, include the death of those we love. A warrior understands that the objective of the battle does not change—but sometimes—the ones on the battlefield will. The Lord, Thy God will never change. He is everlasting. He is The Greatest Comforter. He is The Consoler in your tears. He is your strength when it seems that everything in you is gone. At that point, I encourage you to intentionally pray and fast for God's purpose and His will for you as a widow warrior. His job for you may be so far from anything that you could imagine. Obediently accept it and step into it immediately. Be urgent in your faith. Wherever He takes you is because YOU ARE NEEDED!

FINAL THOUGHTS

My closing remarks is to stand on The Word of God. ABOVE ALL STAND! "Finally, my brethren, be strong in The Lord, and the power of his might. Put on the whole armor of God that ye may be able to stand against the wiles of the devil. For we wrestle not against flesh and blood, but principalities, against powers, against the rulers of the darkness of this world, against spiritual wickedness in high places. Wherefore take unto you the whole armor of God that ye may be able to withstand in the evil day and having done all, to stand. Stand therefore, having your loins girt about with truth, and having on the breastplate of righteousness; And your feet shod with the preparation of the gospel of peace; Above all, taking the shield of faith, wherewith ye shall be able to quench all the fiery darts of the wicked. And take the helmet of salvation, and the sword of the Spirit, which is the Word of God: Praying always with all prayer and supplication in the Spirit, and watching thereunto with all perseverance and supplication for all saints." (Ephesians 6: 10-18)

ABOUT THE AUTHOR

Rosa Lee Walker was born in Brownsville, Tennessee, to Felmer and Bernice Walker. She was the eldest of her siblings. After graduating from Carver High School in Brownsville, TN., in May of 1962, she migrated to the city of New York, a life-long dream. She worked as a nurse's aide for two years, then attended Central School for Practical Nursing, earning a Certificate of Completion in 1965. Three years later, she attended Queensborough Community College, graduating as a Registered Nurse in 1970, with an Associate Degree in Science.

She married the late Robert H. Walker, Jr. in 1971. During their matrimonial bliss, they dedicated three children to The Kingdom of God who are all strong in faith, baptized in Jesus' name, and attended Good Samaritan Apostolic Church. After the death of her husband in 1981, Rosa furthered her education. Answering God's call, Rosa became an evangelist after studying at Bethel Bible Institute in Jamaica, Queens, NY. She received a Certificate in Evangelism in 1982. She graduated from Empire State College with a Bachelor of Science in Gerontology in 1983. As an active member of the Good Samaritan Apostolic Church in Brooklyn, New York, she served in numerous capacities for more than 40 years.

After retirement, Rosa returned to Brownsville, TN where she was ordained as a minister at Christ Temple Apostolic Church. She currently holds various positions: Sunday school teacher, evangelist, and church board member at Christ Temple Apostolic Church. She is also the President of the Bible Willing Workers Ministry in Brownsville, TN. Rosa serves God every day by reading His Word, praying, fasting and encouraging others. She is a role model for her community, church, and family with a servant's heart.

NOTES

All Scripture quotations, unless otherwise indicated, are taken from the King James Version. Super Giant Print, Third Printing, Hendrickson Publishers Edition. Copyright @ May 2020 by Hendrickson Publishers Marketing, LLC.

http://www.The King James Dictionary of Studylight.org Dictionary of Words from the King James Bible. Material presented was supplied by Brandon Staggs and was derived from the KJV Dictionary found on his website located at av1611.com. The unabridged 1828 version of this dictionary in the SwordSearcher Bible Software.

http://www.ninds.nih.gov/disorders/hydrocephalus/detail_hydrocephalus.htm

Mascarenhas, Cynthia. https://walkwithawidow.com/Walk With a Widow: Resources and support for Widows and Widowers.copyrighted 2022.All rights reserved.